my AWESOME Family
THE STORY OF US

YOUR FAMILY'S MEMORIES ARE THE MOST
VALUABLE GIFT YOU CAN GIVE.

FIRST PUBLISHED IN 2017 © LIKE BOOKS & DESIGN LTD 2017
REPRINTED 2019
PRINTED IN CHINA

THIS IS THE STORY OF THE

Family

IT IS A STORY OF THE PAST, OF THE PEOPLE WHO MADE US
AND OF THE MEMORIES WE SHARE.
IT IS A STORY OF THE PRESENT, SO WE'VE LISTED THINGS
WE LOVE TO DO TOGETHER.
IT IS A STORY FOR THE FUTURE, TO PASS ON
TO OUR LOVED ONES.
THIS IS THE STORY OF US.

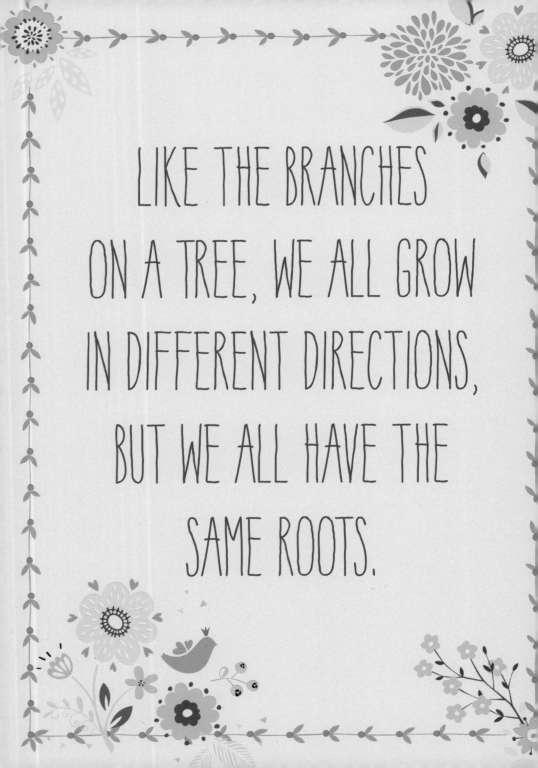

LIKE THE BRANCHES
ON A TREE, WE ALL GROW
IN DIFFERENT DIRECTIONS,
BUT WE ALL HAVE THE
SAME ROOTS.

THIS IS US

Fix photo here

Fill in your name and attach a lovely photo

THIS IS

Fix photo here

POSITION WITHIN THE FAMILY

This next section is all about you

ALL ABOUT ....
Full name

NICKNAME(S) ....

DATE OF BIRTH ....
Including year

I WAS BORN ON A .... AT ....
Day of the week   *Time of day/night*

I WAS BORN AT ....
Home/hospital

I LOOKED LIKE ....
Member of the family

AGE TODAY ....
No fibbing now!

MY FIRST MEMORIES ....

....

....

....

....

MY MUM IS
Full name

MY DAD IS
Full name

BROTHERS & SISTERS
Full name

MY GRANDPARENTS
Full name

OTHER FAMILY MEMBERS
Full name

WHERE I LIVE

....

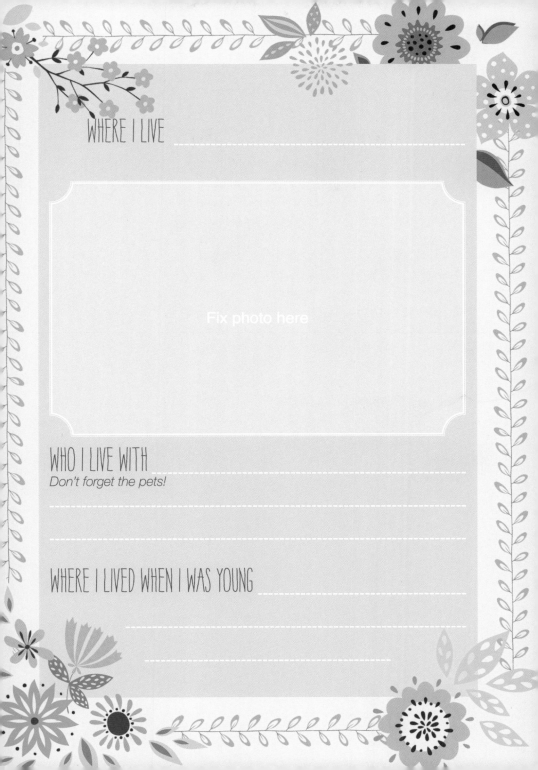

Fix photo here

WHO I LIVE WITH

....

Don't forget the pets!

....

....

WHERE I LIVED WHEN I WAS YOUNG

....

....

....

Happiness
is a family
gathering.

MY TOP 10 FAVOURITE THINGS

Think books, films, songs, sports, places, drink, food and more!

AND A FEW NASTIES

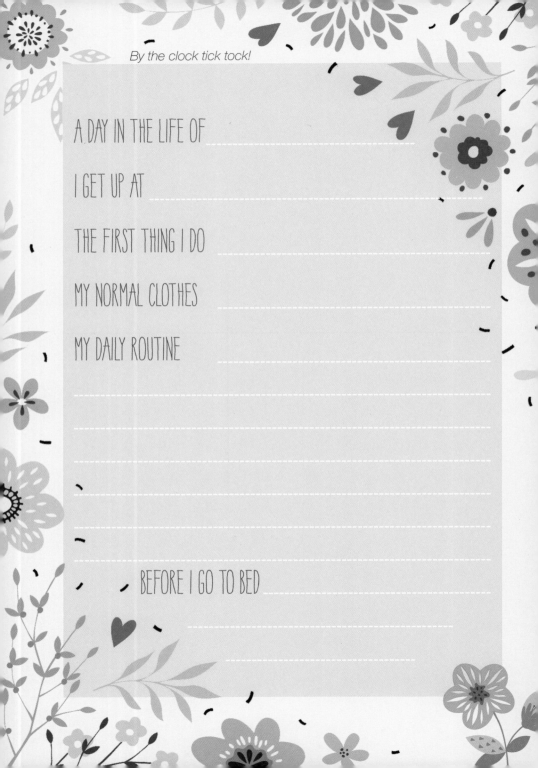

A DAY IN THE LIFE OF ....

I GET UP AT ....

THE FIRST THING I DO ....

MY NORMAL CLOTHES ....

MY DAILY ROUTINE ....

....

....

....

....

BEFORE I GO TO BED ....

....

....

A WEEK IN THE LIFE OF ---------------------------------

MONDAY ---

TUESDAY --

WEDNESDAY ---

THURSDAY --

FRIDAY ---

SATURDAY --

SUNDAY --

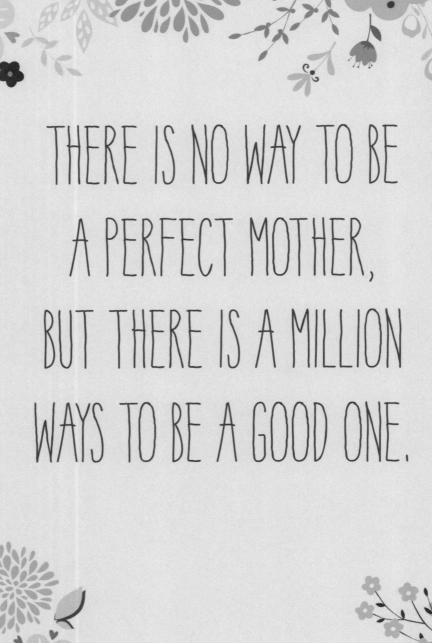

THERE IS NO WAY TO BE A PERFECT MOTHER, BUT THERE IS A MILLION WAYS TO BE A GOOD ONE.

QUICK-FIRE QUESTIONS!

WHAT'S YOUR FAVOURITE COLOUR?

WHAT SUPERPOWER WOULD YOU CHOOSE?

HAVE YOU DANCED IN THE RAIN?

TEA OR COFFEE?

BEST DRESSED MEMBER OF THE FAMILY?

SLEEPING OR RUNNING?

WHAT'S YOUR FAVOURITE ANIMAL?

DO YOU SING IN THE BATH?

WHEN WAS THE LAST TIME YOU LAUGHED?

WHEN WAS THE LAST TIME YOU CRIED?

FUNNIEST MEMBER OF THE FAMILY?

SNOWMAN OR SANDCASTLE?

WHAT'S YOUR PERFECT WAY TO SPEND A DAY?

IF I HAD 3 WISHES THEY WOULD BE

A LETTER TO MY FAMILY

Fill in your name and attach a lovely photo

THIS IS

Fix photo here

POSITION WITHIN THE FAMILY

This next section is all about you

ALL ABOUT
Full name

NICKNAME(S)

DATE OF BIRTH
Including year

I WAS BORN ON A
Day of the week

AT
Time of day/night

I WAS BORN AT
Home/hospital

I LOOKED LIKE
Member of the family

AGE TODAY
No fibbing now!

MY FIRST MEMORIES

MY MUM IS
Full name

MY DAD IS
Full name

BROTHERS & SISTERS
Full name

MY GRANDPARENTS
Full name

OTHER FAMILY MEMBERS
Full name

WHERE I LIVE

....

Fix photo here

WHO I LIVE WITH

Don't forget the pets!

....

....

WHERE I LIVED WHEN I WAS YOUNG

....

....

....

DAD.
A SON'S FIRST HERO
AND A DAUGHTER'S
FIRST LOVE.

MY TOP 10 FAVOURITE THINGS

Think books, films, songs, sports, places, drink, food and more!

AND A FEW NASTIES

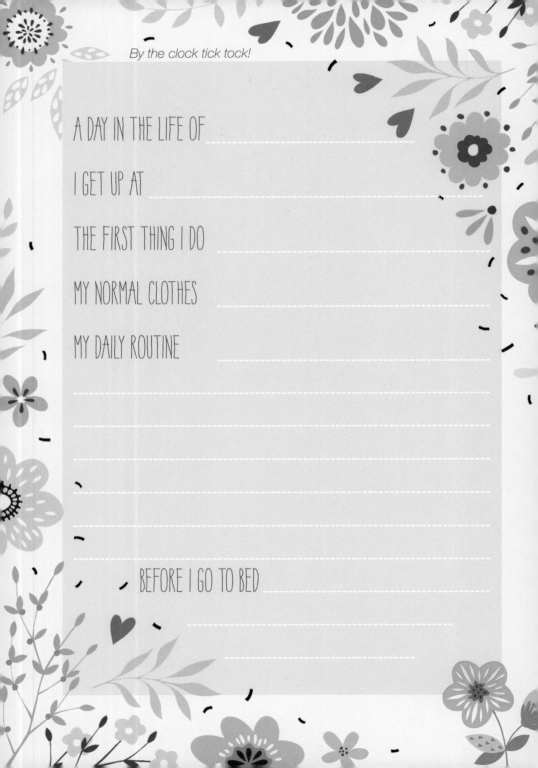

A DAY IN THE LIFE OF _____

I GET UP AT _____

THE FIRST THING I DO _____

MY NORMAL CLOTHES _____

MY DAILY ROUTINE _____

_____

_____

_____

_____

_____

_____

BEFORE I GO TO BED _____

_____

_____

A WEEK IN THE LIFE OF ----------------------------

MONDAY --

TUESDAY --

WEDNESDAY -------------------------------------

THURSDAY ---

FRIDAY ---

SATURDAY --

SUNDAY ---

Family is where

life begins and

love never

ends.

QUICK-FIRE QUESTIONS!

WHAT'S YOUR FAVOURITE COLOUR?

WHAT SUPERPOWER WOULD YOU CHOOSE?

HAVE YOU DANCED IN THE RAIN?

TEA OR COFFEE?

BEST DRESSED MEMBER OF THE FAMILY?

SLEEPING OR RUNNING?

WHAT'S YOUR FAVOURITE ANIMAL?

DO YOU SING IN THE BATH?

WHEN WAS THE LAST TIME YOU LAUGHED?

WHEN WAS THE LAST TIME YOU CRIED?

FUNNIEST MEMBER OF THE FAMILY?

SNOWMAN OR SANDCASTLE?

WHAT'S YOUR PERFECT WAY TO SPEND A DAY?

IF I HAD 3 WISHES THEY WOULD BE

A LETTER TO MY FAMILY

Fill in your name and attach a lovely photo

THIS IS

Fix photo here

POSITION WITHIN THE FAMILY

This next section is all about you

ALL ABOUT
Full name

NICKNAME(S)

DATE OF BIRTH
Including year

I WAS BORN ON A
Day of the week

AT
Time of day/night

I WAS BORN AT
Home/hospital

I LOOKED LIKE
Member of the family

AGE TODAY
No fibbing now!

MY FIRST MEMORIES

MY MUM IS
Full name

MY DAD IS
Full name

BROTHERS & SISTERS
Full name

MY GRANDPARENTS
Full name

OTHER FAMILY MEMBERS
Full name

WHERE I LIVE

Fix photo here

WHO I LIVE WITH

Don't forget the pets!

WHERE I LIVED WHEN I WAS YOUNG

Families
are the
compass
that guide us.

MY TOP 10 FAVOURITE THINGS
Think books, films, songs, sports, places, drink, food and more!

AND A FEW NASTIES

A DAY IN THE LIFE OF

I GET UP AT

THE FIRST THING I DO

MY NORMAL CLOTHES

MY DAILY ROUTINE

BEFORE I GO TO BED

A WEEK IN THE LIFE OF ....

MONDAY ....

....

TUESDAY ....

....

WEDNESDAY ....

....

THURSDAY ....

....

FRIDAY ....

....

SATURDAY ....

....

SUNDAY ....

....

OTHER THINGS MAY CHANGE US, BUT WE START AND END WITH THE FAMILY.

QUICK-FIRE QUESTIONS!

WHAT'S YOUR FAVOURITE COLOUR?

WHAT SUPERPOWER WOULD YOU CHOOSE?

HAVE YOU DANCED IN THE RAIN?

TEA OR COFFEE?

BEST DRESSED MEMBER OF THE FAMILY?

SLEEPING OR RUNNING?

WHAT'S YOUR FAVOURITE ANIMAL?

DO YOU SING IN THE BATH?

WHEN WAS THE LAST TIME YOU LAUGHED?

WHEN WAS THE LAST TIME YOU CRIED?

FUNNIEST MEMBER OF THE FAMILY?

SNOWMAN OR SANDCASTLE?

WHAT'S YOUR PERFECT WAY TO SPEND A DAY?

IF I HAD 3 WISHES THEY WOULD BE

A LETTER TO MY FAMILY

Fill in your name and attach a lovely photo

THIS IS

Fix photo here

POSITION WITHIN THE FAMILY

This next section is all about you

ALL ABOUT
Full name

NICKNAME(S)

DATE OF BIRTH
Including year

I WAS BORN ON A
Day of the week

AT
Time of day/night

I WAS BORN AT
Home/hospital

I LOOKED LIKE
Member of the family

AGE TODAY
No fibbing now!

MY FIRST MEMORIES

MY MUM IS
Full name

MY DAD IS
Full name

BROTHERS & SISTERS
Full name

MY GRANDPARENTS
Full name

OTHER FAMILY MEMBERS
Full name

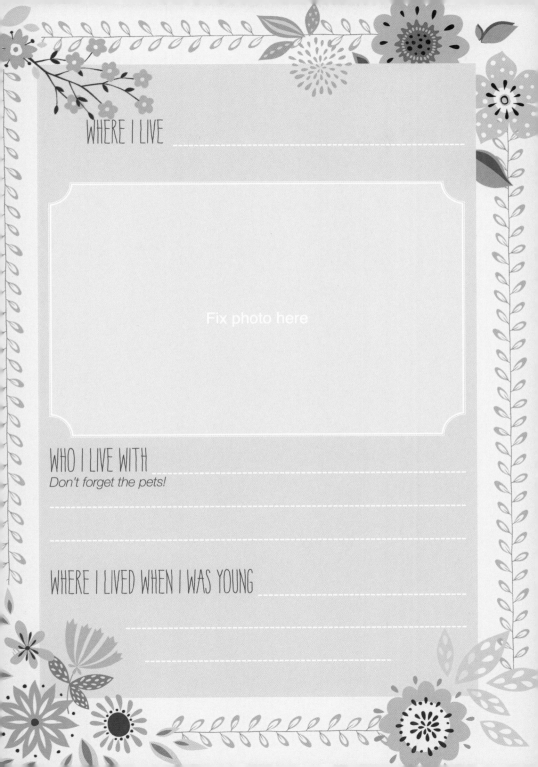

WHERE I LIVE ....

Fix photo here

WHO I LIVE WITH ....

Don't forget the pets!

....

....

WHERE I LIVED WHEN I WAS YOUNG ....

....

....

MY TOP 10 FAVOURITE THINGS
Think books, films, songs, sports, places, drink, food and more!

AND A FEW NASTIES

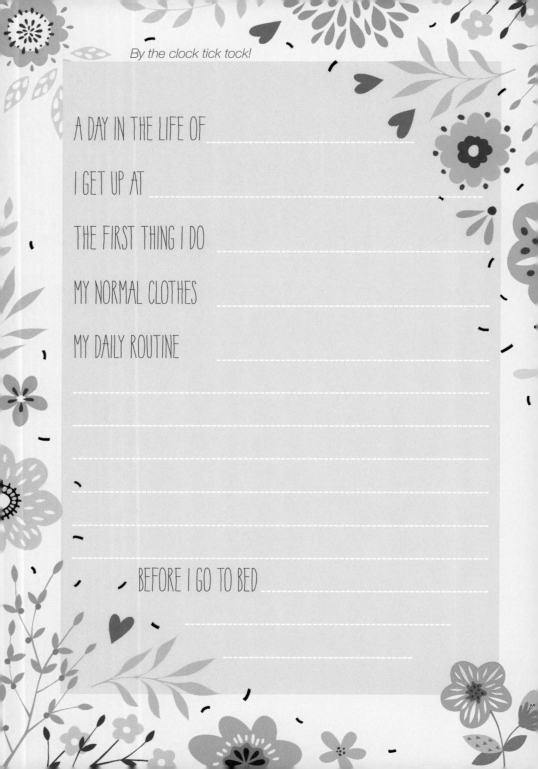

A DAY IN THE LIFE OF ....

I GET UP AT ....

THE FIRST THING I DO ....

MY NORMAL CLOTHES ....

MY DAILY ROUTINE ....

....

....

....

....

....

BEFORE I GO TO BED ....

....

....

A WEEK IN THE LIFE OF ....

MONDAY ....

TUESDAY ....

WEDNESDAY ....

THURSDAY ....

FRIDAY ....

SATURDAY ....

SUNDAY ....

....

MUM.
SHE HOLDS HER CHILD'S
HAND FOR A MOMENT,
AND THEIR HEART
FOR A LIFETIME.

QUICK-FIRE QUESTIONS!

WHAT'S YOUR FAVOURITE COLOUR?

WHAT SUPERPOWER WOULD YOU CHOOSE?

HAVE YOU DANCED IN THE RAIN?

TEA OR COFFEE?

BEST DRESSED MEMBER OF THE FAMILY?

SLEEPING OR RUNNING?

WHAT'S YOUR FAVOURITE ANIMAL?

DO YOU SING IN THE BATH?

WHEN WAS THE LAST TIME YOU LAUGHED?

WHEN WAS THE LAST TIME YOU CRIED?

FUNNIEST MEMBER OF THE FAMILY?

SNOWMAN OR SANDCASTLE?

WHAT'S YOUR PERFECT WAY TO SPEND A DAY?

IF I HAD 3 WISHES THEY WOULD BE

_____

_____

_____

_____

_____

_____

_____

_____

_____

_____

_____

_____

_____

_____

_____

_____

A LETTER TO MY FAMILY

Fill in your name and attach a lovely photo

THIS IS

Fix photo here

POSITION WITHIN THE FAMILY

This next section is all about you

ALL ABOUT
Full name

NICKNAME(S)

DATE OF BIRTH
Including year

I WAS BORN ON A
Day of the week

AT
Time of day/night

I WAS BORN AT
Home/hospital

I LOOKED LIKE
Member of the family

AGE TODAY
No fibbing now!

MY FIRST MEMORIES

MY MUM IS
Full name

MY DAD IS
Full name

BROTHERS & SISTERS
Full name

MY GRANDPARENTS
Full name

OTHER FAMILY MEMBERS
Full name

WHERE I LIVE

Fix photo here

WHO I LIVE WITH

Don't forget the pets!

WHERE I LIVED WHEN I WAS YOUNG

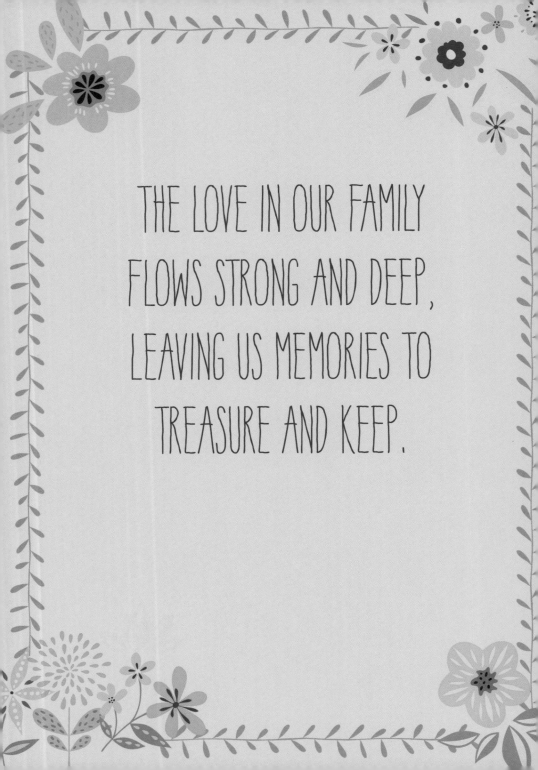

THE LOVE IN OUR FAMILY
FLOWS STRONG AND DEEP,
LEAVING US MEMORIES TO
TREASURE AND KEEP.

MY TOP 10 FAVOURITE THINGS

Think books, films, songs, sports, places, drink, food and more!

AND A FEW NASTIES

A DAY IN THE LIFE OF

I GET UP AT

THE FIRST THING I DO

MY NORMAL CLOTHES

MY DAILY ROUTINE

BEFORE I GO TO BED

A WEEK IN THE LIFE OF ------------------------

MONDAY ------------------------

TUESDAY ------------------------

WEDNESDAY ------------------------

THURSDAY ------------------------

FRIDAY ------------------------

SATURDAY ------------------------

SUNDAY ------------------------

Everyone needs a house to live in, but a supportive family is what builds a home.

QUICK-FIRE QUESTIONS!

WHAT'S YOUR FAVOURITE COLOUR?

WHAT SUPERPOWER WOULD YOU CHOOSE?

HAVE YOU DANCED IN THE RAIN?

TEA OR COFFEE?

BEST DRESSED MEMBER OF THE FAMILY?

SLEEPING OR RUNNING?

WHAT'S YOUR FAVOURITE ANIMAL?

DO YOU SING IN THE BATH?

WHEN WAS THE LAST TIME YOU LAUGHED?

WHEN WAS THE LAST TIME YOU CRIED?

FUNNIEST MEMBER OF THE FAMILY?

SNOWMAN OR SANDCASTLE?

WHAT'S YOUR PERFECT WAY TO SPEND A DAY?

IF I HAD 3 WISHES THEY WOULD BE

A LETTER TO MY FAMILY

Fill in your name and attach a lovely photo

THIS IS

Fix photo here

POSITION WITHIN THE FAMILY

This next section is all about you

ALL ABOUT --
Full name

NICKNAME(S) --

DATE OF BIRTH --
Including year

I WAS BORN ON A ----------------------- AT -------------------
Day of the week   *Time of day/night*

I WAS BORN AT --
Home/hospital

I LOOKED LIKE --
Member of the family

AGE TODAY --
No fibbing now!

MY FIRST MEMORIES --

MY MUM IS
Full name
_____

MY DAD IS
Full name
_____

BROTHERS & SISTERS
Full name
_____

_____

_____

MY GRANDPARENTS
Full name
_____

_____

_____

_____

OTHER FAMILY MEMBERS
Full name
_____

_____

_____

_____

WHERE I LIVE

_____

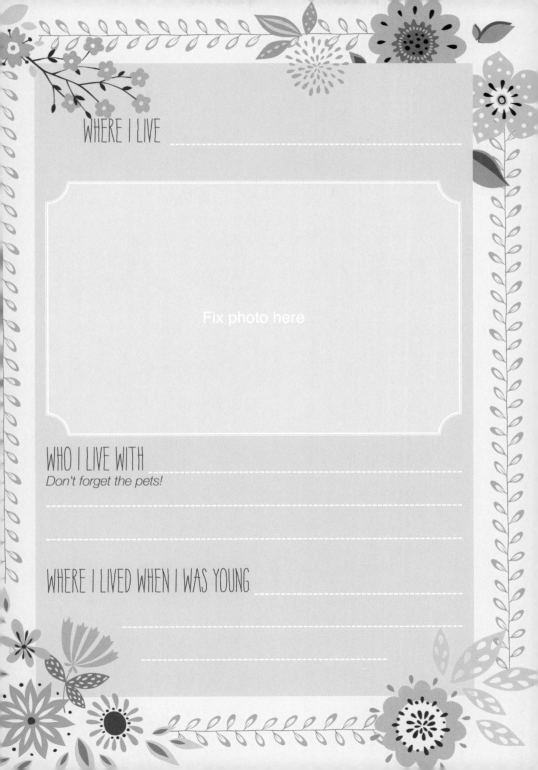

Fix photo here

WHO I LIVE WITH _____
Don't forget the pets!

_____

_____

WHERE I LIVED WHEN I WAS YOUNG _____

_____

_____

Home is where you are loved the most and act the worst.

MY TOP 10 FAVOURITE THINGS

Think books, films, songs, sports, places, drink, food and more!

AND A FEW NASTIES

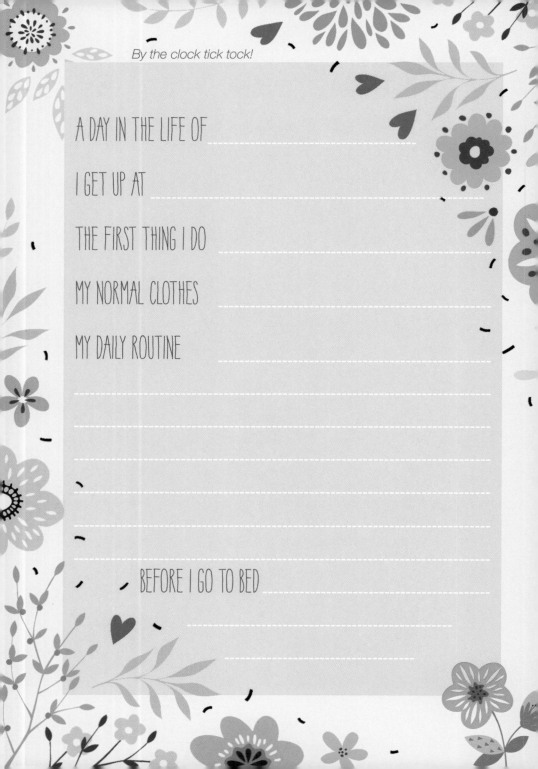

A DAY IN THE LIFE OF ----------------------------------

I GET UP AT --

THE FIRST THING I DO -------------------------------

MY NORMAL CLOTHES ---------------------------------

MY DAILY ROUTINE -----------------------------------

BEFORE I GO TO BED ---------------------------------

A WEEK IN THE LIFE OF ------------------------------

MONDAY ------------------------------

TUESDAY ------------------------------

WEDNESDAY ------------------------------

THURSDAY ------------------------------

FRIDAY ------------------------------

SATURDAY ------------------------------

SUNDAY ------------------------------

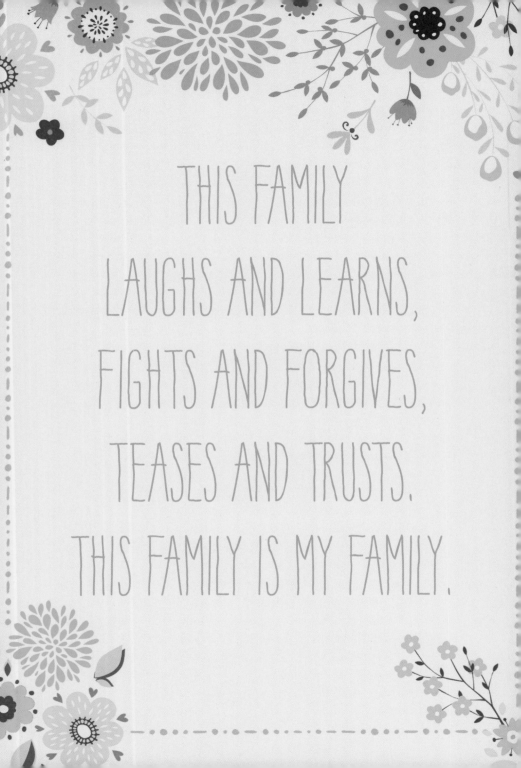

THIS FAMILY
LAUGHS AND LEARNS,
FIGHTS AND FORGIVES,
TEASES AND TRUSTS.
THIS FAMILY IS MY FAMILY.

QUICK-FIRE QUESTIONS!

WHAT'S YOUR FAVOURITE COLOUR?

WHAT SUPERPOWER WOULD YOU CHOOSE?

HAVE YOU DANCED IN THE RAIN?

TEA OR COFFEE?

BEST DRESSED MEMBER OF THE FAMILY?

SLEEPING OR RUNNING?

WHAT'S YOUR FAVOURITE ANIMAL?

DO YOU SING IN THE BATH?

WHEN WAS THE LAST TIME YOU LAUGHED?

WHEN WAS THE LAST TIME YOU CRIED?

FUNNIEST MEMBER OF THE FAMILY?

SNOWMAN OR SANDCASTLE?

WHAT'S YOUR PERFECT WAY TO SPEND A DAY?

IF I HAD 3 WISHES THEY WOULD BE

A LETTER TO MY FAMILY

Fill in your name and attach a lovely photo

THIS IS

Fix photo here

POSITION WITHIN THE FAMILY

This next section is all about you

ALL ABOUT
Full name

NICKNAME(S)

DATE OF BIRTH
Including year

I WAS BORN ON A
Day of the week

AT
Time of day/night

I WAS BORN AT
Home/hospital

I LOOKED LIKE
Member of the family

AGE TODAY
No fibbing now!

MY FIRST MEMORIES

MY MUM IS
Full name

MY DAD IS
Full name

BROTHERS & SISTERS
Full name

MY GRANDPARENTS
Full name

OTHER FAMILY MEMBERS
Full name

WHERE I LIVE

Fix photo here

WHO I LIVE WITH
Don't forget the pets!

WHERE I LIVED WHEN I WAS YOUNG

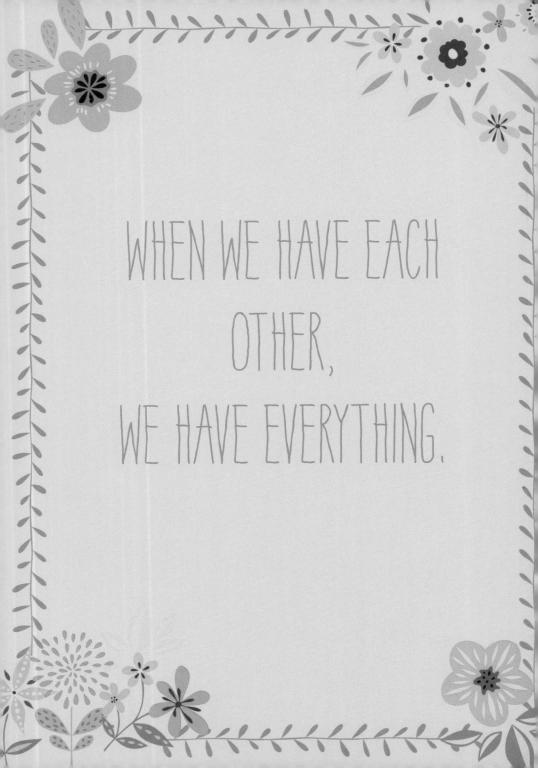

WHEN WE HAVE EACH OTHER,
WE HAVE EVERYTHING.

MY TOP 10 FAVOURITE THINGS

Think books, films, songs, sports, places, drink, food and more!

AND A FEW NASTIES

A DAY IN THE LIFE OF ....

I GET UP AT ....

THE FIRST THING I DO ....

MY NORMAL CLOTHES ....

MY DAILY ROUTINE ....

....

....

....

....

....

.... BEFORE I GO TO BED ....

....

....

A WEEK IN THE LIFE OF --

MONDAY --

TUESDAY --

WEDNESDAY --

THURSDAY --

FRIDAY --

SATURDAY --

SUNDAY --

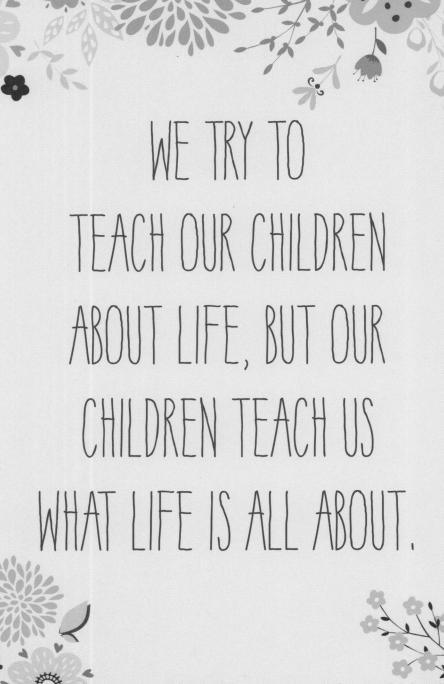

WE TRY TO
TEACH OUR CHILDREN
ABOUT LIFE, BUT OUR
CHILDREN TEACH US
WHAT LIFE IS ALL ABOUT.

QUICK-FIRE QUESTIONS!

WHAT'S YOUR FAVOURITE COLOUR?

WHAT SUPERPOWER WOULD YOU CHOOSE?

HAVE YOU DANCED IN THE RAIN?

TEA OR COFFEE?

BEST DRESSED MEMBER OF THE FAMILY?

SLEEPING OR RUNNING?

WHAT'S YOUR FAVOURITE ANIMAL?

DO YOU SING IN THE BATH?

WHEN WAS THE LAST TIME YOU LAUGHED?

WHEN WAS THE LAST TIME YOU CRIED?

FUNNIEST MEMBER OF THE FAMILY?

SNOWMAN OR SANDCASTLE?

WHAT'S YOUR PERFECT WAY TO SPEND A DAY?

IF I HAD 3 WISHES THEY WOULD BE

A LETTER TO MY FAMILY

Fill in your name and attach a lovely photo

THIS IS

Fix photo here

POSITION WITHIN THE FAMILY

ALL ABOUT
Full name

NICKNAME(S)

DATE OF BIRTH
Including year

I WAS BORN ON A   AT
Day of the week   *Time of day/night*
------------------   ------------------

I WAS BORN AT
Home/hospital

I LOOKED LIKE
Member of the family

AGE TODAY
No fibbing now!

MY FIRST MEMORIES

MY MUM IS ....
Full name

MY DAD IS ....
Full name

BROTHERS & SISTERS ....
Full name

....

MY GRANDPARENTS ....
Full name

....

....

OTHER FAMILY MEMBERS ....
Full name

....

....

....

WHERE I LIVE

....

Fix photo here

WHO I LIVE WITH

....

Don't forget the pets!

....

....

WHERE I LIVED WHEN I WAS YOUNG

....

....

....

Family – a link
to the past
and a bridge to
the future.

MY TOP 10 FAVOURITE THINGS
Think books, films, songs, sports, places, drink, food and more!

AND A FEW NASTIES

A DAY IN THE LIFE OF --------------------------

I GET UP AT --------------------------------

THE FIRST THING I DO --------------------

MY NORMAL CLOTHES --------------------

MY DAILY ROUTINE --------------------

BEFORE I GO TO BED --------------------

A WEEK IN THE LIFE OF _____

MONDAY _____

TUESDAY _____

WEDNESDAY _____

THURSDAY _____

FRIDAY _____

SATURDAY _____

SUNDAY _____

Family - we
may not have
it all together,
but together we
have it all.

QUICK-FIRE QUESTIONS!

WHAT'S YOUR FAVOURITE COLOUR?

WHAT SUPERPOWER WOULD YOU CHOOSE?

HAVE YOU DANCED IN THE RAIN?

TEA OR COFFEE?

BEST DRESSED MEMBER OF THE FAMILY?

SLEEPING OR RUNNING?

WHAT'S YOUR FAVOURITE ANIMAL?

DO YOU SING IN THE BATH?

WHEN WAS THE LAST TIME YOU LAUGHED?

WHEN WAS THE LAST TIME YOU CRIED?

FUNNIEST MEMBER OF THE FAMILY?

SNOWMAN OR SANDCASTLE?

WHAT'S YOUR PERFECT WAY TO SPEND A DAY?

IF I HAD 3 WISHES THEY WOULD BE

_____

_____

_____

_____

_____

_____

_____

_____

_____

_____

_____

_____

_____

_____

_____

_____

A LETTER TO MY FAMILY

Fill in your name and attach a lovely photo

THIS IS

Fix photo here

POSITION WITHIN THE FAMILY

This next section is all about you

ALL ABOUT
Full name

NICKNAME(S)

DATE OF BIRTH
Including year

I WAS BORN ON A
Day of the week

AT
Time of day/night

I WAS BORN AT
Home/hospital

I LOOKED LIKE
Member of the family

AGE TODAY
No fibbing now!

MY FIRST MEMORIES

MY MUM IS
Full name --

MY DAD IS
Full name --

BROTHERS & SISTERS
Full name --

MY GRANDPARENTS
Full name --

OTHER FAMILY MEMBERS
Full name --

WHERE I LIVE

....

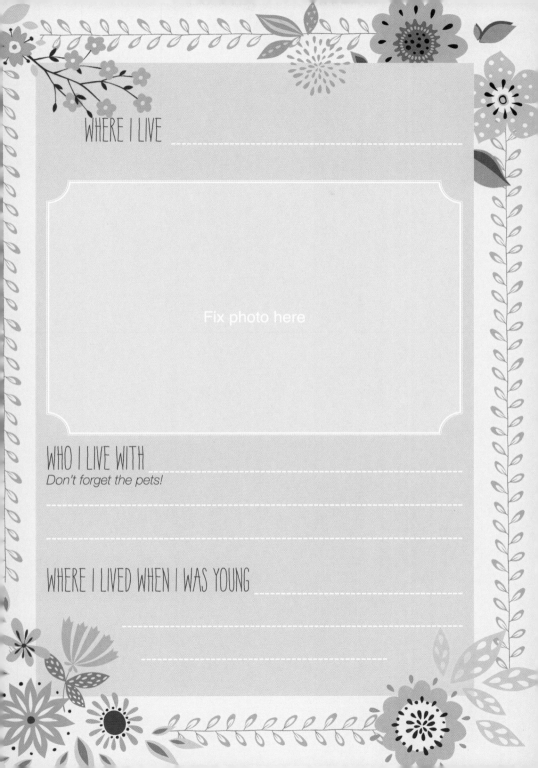

Fix photo here

WHO I LIVE WITH

Don't forget the pets!

....

....

WHERE I LIVED WHEN I WAS YOUNG

....

....

....

FAMILY IS NOT
AN IMPORTANT THING.
IT'S EVERYTHING.

MY TOP 10 FAVOURITE THINGS

Think books, films, songs, sports, places, drink, food and more!

AND A FEW NASTIES

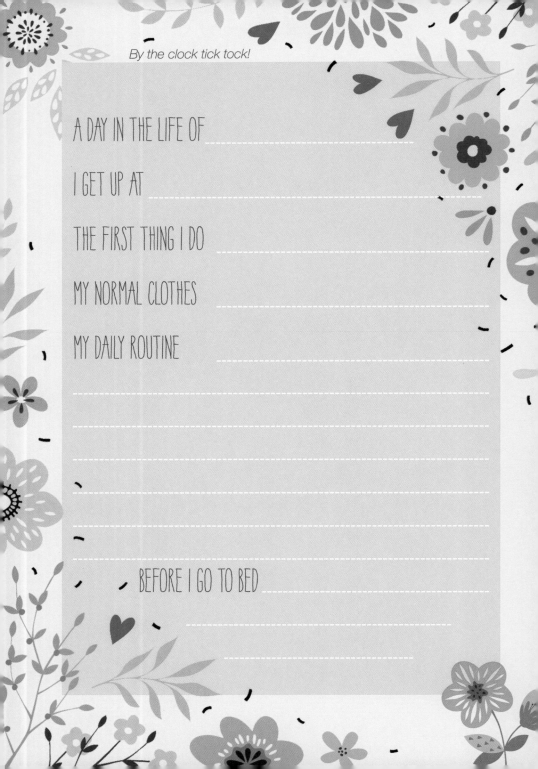

A DAY IN THE LIFE OF _____

I GET UP AT _____

THE FIRST THING I DO _____

MY NORMAL CLOTHES _____

MY DAILY ROUTINE _____

_____

_____

_____

_____

_____

BEFORE I GO TO BED _____

_____

_____

A WEEK IN THE LIFE OF ------------------------

MONDAY ------------------------------------

TUESDAY ----------------------------------

WEDNESDAY --------------------------------

THURSDAY ---------------------------------

FRIDAY -----------------------------------

SATURDAY ---------------------------------

SUNDAY -----------------------------------

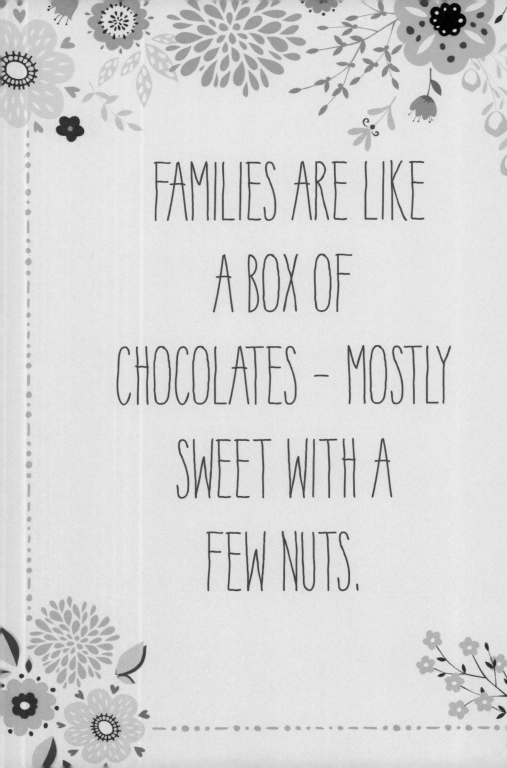

FAMILIES ARE LIKE
A BOX OF
CHOCOLATES – MOSTLY
SWEET WITH A
FEW NUTS.

QUICK-FIRE QUESTIONS!

WHAT'S YOUR FAVOURITE COLOUR?

WHAT SUPERPOWER WOULD YOU CHOOSE?

HAVE YOU DANCED IN THE RAIN?

TEA OR COFFEE?

BEST DRESSED MEMBER OF THE FAMILY?

SLEEPING OR RUNNING?

WHAT'S YOUR FAVOURITE ANIMAL?

DO YOU SING IN THE BATH?

WHEN WAS THE LAST TIME YOU LAUGHED?

WHEN WAS THE LAST TIME YOU CRIED?

FUNNIEST MEMBER OF THE FAMILY?

SNOWMAN OR SANDCASTLE?

WHAT'S YOUR PERFECT WAY TO SPEND A DAY?

IF I HAD 3 WISHES THEY WOULD BE

A LETTER TO MY FAMILY

Fill in your name and attach a lovely photo

THIS IS

Fix photo here

POSITION WITHIN THE FAMILY

This next section is all about you

ALL ABOUT
Full name

NICKNAME(S)

DATE OF BIRTH
Including year

I WAS BORN ON A
Day of the week

AT
Time of day/night

I WAS BORN AT
Home/hospital

I LOOKED LIKE
Member of the family

AGE TODAY
No fibbing now!

MY FIRST MEMORIES

MY MUM IS
Full name

MY DAD IS
Full name

BROTHERS & SISTERS
Full name

MY GRANDPARENTS
Full name

OTHER FAMILY MEMBERS
Full name

WHERE I LIVE

_____

Fix photo here

WHO I LIVE WITH _____
Don't forget the pets!

_____

_____

WHERE I LIVED WHEN I WAS YOUNG _____

_____

_____

Brothers and
sisters share
childhood
memories and
grown up
dreams.

MY TOP 10 FAVOURITE THINGS

Think books, films, songs, sports, places, drink, food and more!

AND A FEW NASTIES

A DAY IN THE LIFE OF ----------------------------------

I GET UP AT ----------------------------------

THE FIRST THING I DO ----------------------------------

MY NORMAL CLOTHES ----------------------------------

MY DAILY ROUTINE ----------------------------------

BEFORE I GO TO BED ----------------------------------

A WEEK IN THE LIFE OF

MONDAY

TUESDAY

WEDNESDAY

THURSDAY

FRIDAY

SATURDAY

SUNDAY

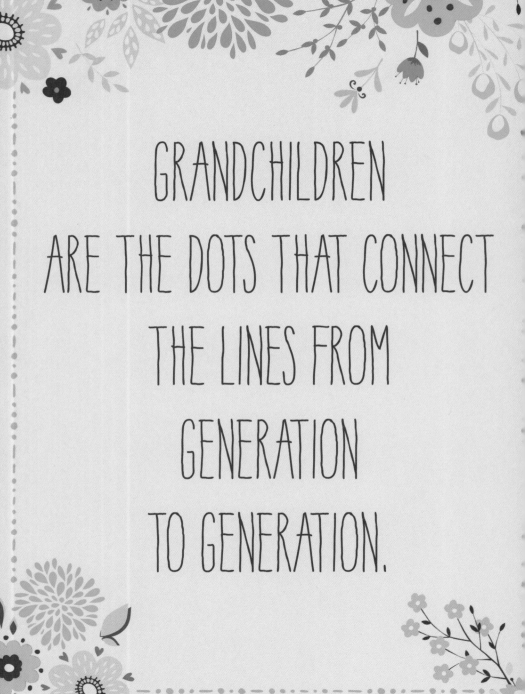

GRANDCHILDREN
ARE THE DOTS THAT CONNECT
THE LINES FROM
GENERATION
TO GENERATION.

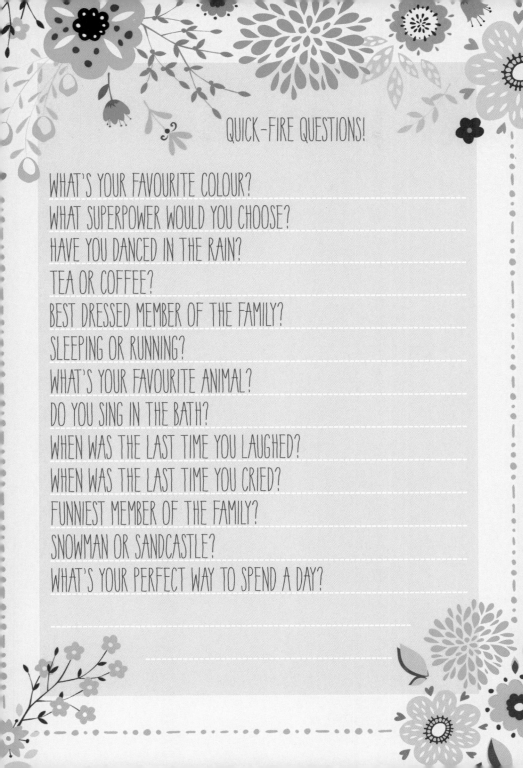

QUICK-FIRE QUESTIONS!

WHAT'S YOUR FAVOURITE COLOUR?

WHAT SUPERPOWER WOULD YOU CHOOSE?

HAVE YOU DANCED IN THE RAIN?

TEA OR COFFEE?

BEST DRESSED MEMBER OF THE FAMILY?

SLEEPING OR RUNNING?

WHAT'S YOUR FAVOURITE ANIMAL?

DO YOU SING IN THE BATH?

WHEN WAS THE LAST TIME YOU LAUGHED?

WHEN WAS THE LAST TIME YOU CRIED?

FUNNIEST MEMBER OF THE FAMILY?

SNOWMAN OR SANDCASTLE?

WHAT'S YOUR PERFECT WAY TO SPEND A DAY?

IF I HAD 3 WISHES THEY WOULD BE

A LETTER TO MY FAMILY

Behind every young child who follows a dream, is a parent who gave them a map.

JANUARY
Birthday, celebrations and special days!

1ST	2ND	3RD	4TH	5TH
6TH	7TH	8TH	9TH	10TH	11TH
12TH	13TH	14TH	15TH	16TH	17TH
18TH	19TH	20TH	21ST	22ND	23RD
24TH	25TH	26TH	27TH	28TH	29TH
30TH	31ST				

NOTES

FEBRUARY

Birthday, celebrations and special days!

1ST	2ND	3RD	4TH	5TH	6TH
7TH	8TH	9TH	10TH	11TH	12TH
13TH	14TH	15TH	16TH	17TH	18TH
19TH	20TH	21ST	21ND	23RD	24TH
25TH	26TH	27TH	28TH	29TH	

NOTES

MARCH

Birthday, celebrations and special days!

1ST	2ND	3RD	4TH	5TH	6TH
7TH	8TH	9TH	10TH	11TH	12TH
13TH	14TH	15TH	16TH	17TH	18TH
19TH	20TH	21ST	22ND	23RD	24TH
25TH	26TH	27TH	28TH	29TH	30TH

31ST

NOTES

APRIL

Birthday, celebrations and special days!

1ST	2ND	3RD	4TH	5TH	6TH
7TH	8TH	9TH	10TH	11TH	12TH
13TH	14TH	15TH	16TH	17TH	18TH
19TH	20TH	21ST	22ND	23RD	24TH
25TH	26TH	27TH	28TH	29TH	30TH

NOTES

THE FACES OF OUR FAMILY
ARE MAGIC MIRRORS
SHOWING US THE PAST,
PRESENT AND FUTURE.

MAY

Birthday, celebrations and special days!

1ST	2ND	3RD	4TH	5TH	6TH
7TH	8TH	9TH	10TH	11TH	12TH
13TH	14TH	15TH	16TH	17TH	18TH
19TH	20TH	21ST	22ND	23RD	24TH
25TH	26TH	27TH	28TH	29TH	30TH

31ST	NOTES

_____

_____

_____

JUNE

Birthday, celebrations and special days!

1ST	2ND	3RD	4TH	5TH	6TH
7TH	8TH	9TH	10TH	11TH	12TH
13TH	14TH	15TH	16TH	17TH	18TH
19TH	20TH	21ST	22ND	23RD	24TH
25TH	26TH	27TH	28TH	29TH	30TH

NOTES

....

....

....

....

....

JULY
Birthday, celebrations and special days!

1ST	2ND	3RD	4TH	5TH
6TH	7TH	8TH	9TH	10TH	11TH
12TH	13TH	14TH	15TH	16TH	17TH
18TH	19TH	20TH	21ST	22ND	23RD
24TH	25TH	26TH	27TH	28TH	29TH
30TH	31ST			

NOTES

AUGUST

Birthday, celebrations and special days!

1ST	2ND	3RD	4TH	5TH	6TH
7TH	8TH	9TH	10TH	11TH	12TH
13TH	14TH	15TH	16TH	17TH	18TH
19TH	20TH	21ST	22ND	23RD	24TH
25TH	26TH	27TH	28TH	29TH	30TH

31ST

NOTES

SEPTEMBER

Birthday, celebrations and special days!

1ST	2ND	3RD	4TH	5TH	6TH
7TH	8TH	9TH	10TH	11TH	12TH
13TH	14TH	15TH	16TH	17TH	18TH
19TH	20TH	21ST	22ND	23RD	24TH
25TH	26TH	27TH	28TH	29TH	30TH

NOTES

OCTOBER

Birthday, celebrations and special days!

1ST	2ND	3RD	4TH	5TH	6TH
7TH	8TH	9TH	10TH	11TH	12TH
13TH	14TH	15TH	16TH	17TH	18TH
19TH	20TH	21ST	22ND	23RD	24TH
25TH	26TH	27TH	28TH	29TH	30TH

31ST

NOTES

NOVEMBER

Birthday, celebrations and special days!

1ST	2ND	3RD	4TH	5TH	6TH
7TH	8TH	9TH	10TH	11TH	12TH
13TH	14TH	15TH	16TH	17TH	18TH
19TH	20TH	21ST	22ND	23RD	24TH
25TH	26TH	27TH	28TH	29TH	30TH

NOTES

_____

_____

_____

_____

_____

DECEMBER

Birthday, celebrations and special days!

1ST	2ND	3RD	4TH	5TH	6TH
7TH	8TH	9TH	10TH	11TH	12TH
13TH	14TH	15TH	16TH	17TH	18TH
19TH	20TH	21ST	22ND	23RD	24TH
25TH	26TH	27TH	28TH	29TH	30TH

31ST	NOTES

FUN TIMES WE'VE HAD

Holidays, days out (and days in!)

WHERE _____

WHEN _____

WHO WITH _____

Fix photo here

MEMORIES _____

_____

_____

_____

_____

FUN TIMES WE'VE HAD

Holidays, days out (and days in!)

WHERE _____

WHEN _____

WHO WITH _____

Fix photo here

MEMORIES _____

_____

_____

_____

_____

FUN TIMES WE'VE HAD

Holidays, days out (and days in!)

WHERE ....

WHEN ....

WHO WITH ....

Fix photo here

MEMORIES ....

....

....

....

....

FUN TIMES WE'VE HAD

Holidays, days out (and days in!)

WHERE ....

WHEN ....

WHO WITH ....

Fix photo here

MEMORIES ....

....

....

....

....

FUN TIMES WE'VE HAD

Holidays, days out (and days in!)

WHERE ....

WHEN ....

WHO WITH

Fix photo here

MEMORIES ....

....

....

....

....

FUN TIMES WE'VE HAD

Holidays, days out (and days in!)

WHERE ....

WHEN ....

WHO WITH ....

Fix photo here

MEMORIES

....

....

....

....

FUN TIMES WE'VE HAD

Holidays, days out (and days in!)

WHERE ....

WHEN ....

WHO WITH ....

Fix photo here

MEMORIES ....

....

....

....

FUN TIMES WE'VE HAD

Holidays, days out (and days in!)

WHERE

WHEN

WHO WITH

Fix photo here

MEMORIES

FUN TIMES WE'VE HAD
Holidays, days out (and days in!)

WHERE _____

WHEN _____

WHO WITH _____

Fix photo here

MEMORIES _____

_____

_____

_____

_____

FUN TIMES WE'VE HAD
Holidays, days out (and days in!)

WHERE ....

WHEN ....

WHO WITH ....

Fix photo here

MEMORIES

....

....

....

....

....

BEING A FAMILY MEANS YOU ARE PART OF SOMETHING WONDERFUL. YOU WILL LOVE AND BE LOVED FOR THE REST OF YOUR LIFE.

WE'RE ALL AWESOME

Here are a few amazing awards and achievements

WHO ....

ACHIEVEMENT ....

DATE ....

Fix photo here

MEMORIES ....

....

....

....

....

WE'RE ALL AWESOME

Here are a few amazing awards and achievements

WHO ....

ACHIEVEMENT ....

DATE ....

Fix photo here

MEMORIES ....

....

....

....

....

WE'RE ALL AWESOME

Here are a few amazing awards and achievements

WHO _____

ACHIEVEMENT _____

DATE _____

Fix photo here

MEMORIES _____

_____

_____

_____

_____

WE'RE ALL AWESOME

Here are a few amazing awards and achievements

WHO ....

ACHIEVEMENT ....

DATE ....

Fix photo here

MEMORIES ....

....

....

....

WE'RE ALL AWESOME

Here are a few amazing awards and achievements

WHO
ACHIEVEMENT
DATE

Fix photo here

MEMORIES

WE'RE ALL AWESOME

Here are a few amazing awards and achievements

WHO

ACHIEVEMENT

DATE

Fix photo here

MEMORIES

THINGS THAT WE ARE THANKFUL FOR

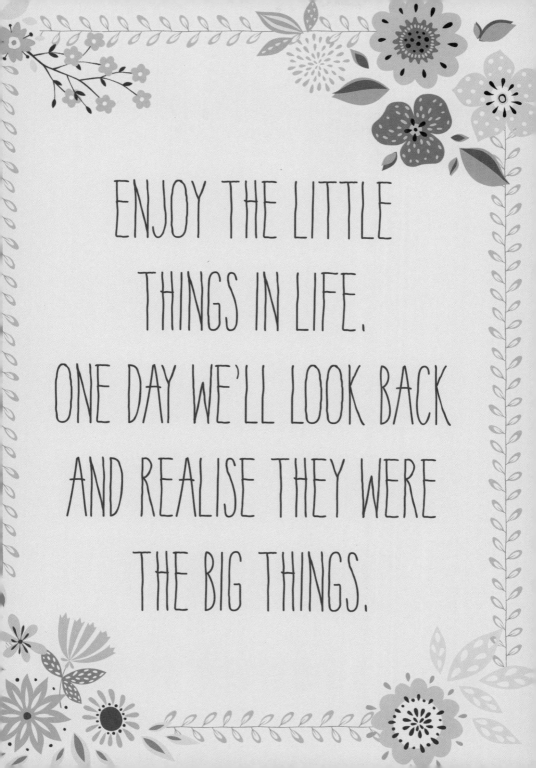

ENJOY THE LITTLE
THINGS IN LIFE.
ONE DAY WE'LL LOOK BACK
AND REALISE THEY WERE
THE BIG THINGS.

GOODBYE FROM US

Fix photo here

COMPLETED WITH LOVE BY THE MEMBERS OF THE FAMILY ON